A PHIAL OF PASSING MEMORIES

A Phial of Passing Memories

James Yékú

poems

MAWENZI
HOUSE

We acknowledge the support of the Canada Council for the Arts for our publishing program. We also acknowledge support from the Government of Ontario through the Ontario Arts Council, and the support of the Government of Canada through the Canada Book Fund.

ONTARIO ARTS COUNCIL
CONSEIL DES ARTS DE L'ONTARIO
an Ontario government agency
un organisme du gouvernement de l'Ontario
Ontario
Canada Council for the Arts
Conseil des arts du Canada
Canada

Cover design by Babatunde Idowu-Taylor

Library and Archives Canada Cataloguing in Publication

Title: A phial of passing memories : poems / James Yékú.

Names: Yékú, James, author

Identifiers: Canadiana (print) 20250164507 | Canadiana (ebook) 20250164612 | ISBN 9781774151921 (softcover) | ISBN 9781774151938 (EPUB) | ISBN 9781774151945 (PDF)

Subjects: LCGFT: Poetry.

Classification: LCC PS8647.E49 P45 2025 | DDC C811/.6—dc23

Printed and bound in Canada by Coach House Printing

Mawenzi House Publishers
192 Spadina Ave, Suite 417
Toronto, ON, M5T 2C2
Canada

www.mawenzihouse.com

For Kemi, in whose eyes a thousand bougainvilleas sway
hesitant lips into a symphony of breathless desires

Contents

I

II

III

IV

V

I

In Shifting Scapes

poetry wanders,
meandering into
a sail with itself

like a flâneur, mixing a child's curiosity with
the sights of strangers smiling indifferent
hellos to friends on a busy Paris street.

One November, the rain was a rogue
that poured like a mischief-maker
determined to bury the city in a field of tides.

    The roar of its waters mortified the weather bots
    that swore a cloudy sky was no threat to the road
    until the crossroads chief arrived with chaos and pranks.

  Even now as he chases jaunts,
  eternity abides neither there nor here,
  for as daily wanderings beckon to us,
    as a peripatetic flinching
      for all things strange and sane,
        so do the memories
          we collect of them:

  the scars of conflicts,
the masks of love,
          and the weft of forbidden pleasures
      between
the wandering legs of troubadours.

Poetry reclaims its wonder in *shifting scapes,*
and the Baedeker resumes its travels,
with ambivalence vanishing into
the known and unknowable.

These poems wander too, mixing a child's
curiosity with the sights of strangers smiling
indifferent hellos on streets bursting
with fleeting memories *phialed* from rivers
overflowing their banks like the Seine.

An Opening Glee

As she finished pushing
during a birth in Berlin,

where it was winter
and a warm hospital
ward was spilling out life;

and newborns cried
to a midwife's chants
and welcome;

then she swaddled
him, skin touching skin—

an opening glee in
the drama of first
affections,

the pride of her eyes,
fastened on him:

the arms, the legs,
and the half-open
eyes staring back
in vague familiarity;

making contact
was natural:

the smoothness
of his skin and
the softness of a tiny
sweetness draped
in vernix

mixed with the prayers
of a new mother
into a tapestry love.

A Toddler's Goodbye

It was the last day of school for her that spring,
and it seemed the unfurling of farewells among
ladybugs and pluvious eyes could be a theater
of dreams, with toddlers on Lawrence's hilltop
the audiences of their own play—arms that wrap
tightly around a preschooler, like a final rite
in a room of treasures, toys, and giggles.

I was there, too, a smiling observer in the play
of innocence. It was the last day before the flight
from O'Hare, and some tiny footfalls were departing
into the dance of a difficult goodbye.
Like the pitter-patters of restive feet, the pathos
of the moment came like a poem that needed
to be written, but so did a heavy sigh bearing
joys that made a response unthinkable.

And then it happened again at *Kita*:
it was the last day of school for her that spring,
and an avalanche of warmth triggered some
merry *tschüss*: "I will miss you, Eva,"
a *lehrerin* leading the chorus of kids who may
never remember the time they had together.

A Digital Memorial

The other day I watched a friend's piercing words
break through the crowded wall of a mutual
on Facebook. It was a tribute to a fondness past,
to a soul disappeared into the memories of photos,
events and birthday messages they will never read.
I scrolled through a frozen timeline, the coldness
of it all like a lonely grave lined with orchids and lilies.
Then a comment caught my eye, and then
another, both written by friends of the departed
to wish them a long and prosperous life.
Those comments did not gather a storm of likes
nor summoned a sheen for the parade of egos,
only plaintive sighs for the festival of fleeting beings.
But I wondered if someone beyond our realm
was reading the affections of earthlings,
flipping through each post before tossing
them into the void until they reached
my constricted heart.

Ìwàlẹwà

Talent presented itself to those chasing
the lores of other delights. Its strains
called out again to them that morning, to
folks avoiding it the most; it was the time
of the cherry blossoms, and its melodies
ricocheted through the walls of an old
kitchen in East Berlin. But that didn't
matter to them. Yet, the girl played on,
calling music to the memories of love;
on the edge of a bench, back straight, her eyes
glinted with the mischief of an expert,
her hands fingering the Viennese piano
in the adjoining room in a mixture
of dreams and chords, a harmonic tune
to seduce bemused ears into dreamscapes
bustling with ardor. Still, a shower of praise
did not pour. Nor did applauses to crown
the muse that set a soul on jubilant fires.
So, she sauntered through the kitchen, startled
by the indifference of an unfeeling audience.
"Good job, Ìwàlẹwà," the haste of the words
betraying the iridescence of a face feigning anger.
She stormed back to her player, bringing to life
a familiar anthem, the ghost of *Danny Boy*.
It was then the stirrings began, spectral sounds
that summoned the hopes of those pining
for union with what is gone and what is to come.

All My Friends Have Left Home

All my friends have left home.
One left his PhD to sell ice at Walmart,
after he fled the heat of a laboratory
without microscopes, another the lushness
of Banana Island in search of himself
in the frigidness of lands quivering
with desire for cheap labor.

A childhood favorite floods my WhatsApp
with images that burn with rage:
the remains of a life vanished by stray
bullets that fling dreams away.

He too has kissed mother a final time,
his goodbyes fading into the assurances
of strangers who promise a passage
through hell. He tells me the girl
we both wanted was last seen in Kuwait,
her passport seized by princes whose
feet and pipe she must daily kiss.

All my friends have left home;
others become robots, preferring
the opium of honey-tongue pastors
who promise a heaven in the infernos
of Lagos, the ruins of a megacity
built for the rich.

All my friends have left home,
some to Canada, others to Canterbury—
where timber-framed streets welcome
tired legs of dust. But some find hope again:

in the smiles of deceptive border agents
and the lukewarm welcome of an open-door
society overrun by the eager feet of new
arrivals bearing a litany of broken sighs
at the sight of their new home.

An Old House on Main

Beside a rusty fire hydrant on the corner
of Main in Saskatoon stands a house belonging
to the new arrivals, illegals the locals call them,
whose delights overthrow the tantrums of
a weathered building staled with the lines of age,
a building stained with the desires of those
longing for more of something unknown.

The soberness of its quaint door, a memorial
to the forgetting of freedom; its colors betray
like a passion, flames refusing to be fanned.
It is not the house you dream of before you
leave your paradise in Porto-Novo. Yet, it
welcomes your tired feet, sheltering
them from the gathering dust.

This house welcomes the dreams you bring
to be reborn in the new world, a world that
does not see you. You may seek in its face
a second home to remind you of a house
beyond the Atlantic, beyond the house
of history's angel, his gaze fixed on the past,
whose music dances to ruins of empty time.

This house, a pile of debris, becomes both
a storm and a farce, as Benjamin saw,
a progress for those vanquished by power,
for those for whom a building is both a
developer's ruins and a refuge of hope.

Afrofuturist Sankofa

The gemstones of times to come
rebelling against the afterlives
of homochromatic violence belong
in the loins of the ancients, ancestors
of the future who heal with their words
and rain down wisdom from the loft
of sacred trees from which they
sprout rocket cities and resilience.
Humanoids, too, metal mortals from
distant clans who parade their truth
as brothers in our new galaxies.
Each night, I look above to touch their smile.
Each night, I seek the scents of their senses,
lurch into the place where becoming Black
is a delight to the earth, where the shadow
of freedom provides the sureties of liberties
once denied by those who swore most to
the sacraments of ethics and equality.
Perhaps I will be lucky to see the world
to come, to sit with Malcolm and Mandela,
fraternal sages for the fellowship of the free,
in whose breasts holy fire dwells with flames
of harmony. But to surrender myself to
this languor and the wistfulness it calls within
me is to negate their memories, the triumphs
of elders—alive again to guide our sail
to Mars, to the heart of the Orishas, whose
lights are emissaries from the herbs

and fountain we drink to life.
So, as one that retrieves a daughter
forgotten in the march of progress, I stand
here, a supplicant before a willful deity,
beseeching the moons to unfold the
hidden scrolls of history and code their
struggles into the spirit of the Panthers,
into the souls of their architectures
and dreams. With eyes that cover the earth,
that look back to the future, I, Sankofa—
sage bard of the crimson skies—dance
with them and the unborn to the drums of
artifices, engines powered by the graces
of Black souls.

Existentialist

Sometimes you're convinced life is a cracked cistern
in which you pour passions and an endless tale of toils
as a motion that vanishes into a profound nothingness.

Like a tangled pocket with a hole, it is the abyss
of your most chiseled shadows, the abode
of the emptiness that haunts the soul.

A loveless life is nothing but a basket of water
in a Sahara of thirst, a desolate sea of wilderness
from which might flow a bubbling spring

if love satiates as an infinite rush of water,
a serein which, from cloudless skies,
refreshes beyond the enclosures of time.

What then is *this* life, God, if not the river that flows
from naught within your heart, bringing verse
and life that quilt beauty from a meaningless void?

Sometimes, you're convinced of this;
other times, not so.

A Flight

There is a fight in every bird to know itself,
to contemplate the pirouettes of its rustling
feathers and the myths of freedoms that vanish
into an endless flight of wings outstretched
to the gales of a mirrored existence.

One autumn morn as the sun burst out
on a cloudy hill in a Lawrence manor,
a red robin by the glass window returned
to behold itself, a communion between
the bird and his reflection, threaded by the hands
of nature into an embroidery of marvel and strength.

Each struggle against the glass was
an unending fight of nothingness; each struggle,
a ceaseless charge against the shadows of the self.

As the robin went against its silhouette,
the weight of a massive boulder we all
struggle to carry became its comfort.

A Death Retold in Solitude

His eyes, now a garden of gloom, once budded flowers
that brought near those that are gone like the winds
of time. He was in the twilight of life, when sleep came
more often than he wanted, and the slowness
of age fancied the energy of a boy.

And there he lay one night, musing on the swiftness of it all,
the shortness of a long journey about to end, his thoughts
lingering on the life that was floating away and whatever
it was that made living tolerable.

It didn't matter, a hermit without worldly cares,
that solitude was his only companion; to die alone was never
a choice he made himself. Yet, the day he left came without
any whimper, as uneventful as the life he wished he had lived.

That night, there were neither tears nor dread, nobody to hold
his hands and whisper courage as he slipped into a timeless void.
Except a light from elsewhere, shining to record the grayness
of a faded smile in the phial of his passing memories.

Power Dunk

Everyone has got a little cave
in which they feel seen, sturdy
like a stream that cuts through rocks,
desiring fame for the river it feeds.

Oftentimes,
        the tides of
                life push us
away from our cave, causing us to wander
like Ajala, far from its familiar anchor.

We may sometimes meet another
who, in their role as a sovereign
of all barren lands and seas, rides over
us like the anger of wind in a storm
of ego, who subdues from their hole
and makes some tremble and strut
under their whims and yoke;
we may meet another, a wannabe god
overflowing with illusion and violence.

But everyone soon returns to their nest
where they recover the power lost
elsewhere—the warmth of those who
see us again and never break us.

Grief

that limns the face when, on TikTok, we witness the carnage
of war compares little

to the pathos of those for whom horror sculpts a breathing
hashtag, casualties

for whom the revulsions of the rocket sing of the paths to life,
the final rite before

a macabre dance in the fields of hypocrisy. For us upon whom
the bullets rain,

and the flames of unceasing fire burn like a cannon in the
hands of a beloved foe,

the images of war are never simulacra, ever a terror that stalks
those who are the dying.

A Fevered World Cup

I

So, the desert sky would not welcome him,
his life threaded by the chains of a Kafala weaver.
A dusty cloud looming over him like the threat
of skylines sprawling the roads to Olympic stadiums
blossomed from the beads of his sweat.

An outcast among tourists and fans, untouchable,
as a leper who wears shame like the jersey
of a keeper who lets in a barrage of goals.

They passed by him without a glance,
their gaze focused on the digital billboard
splashing images of Messi and Ronaldo
juggling a ball in a #Saynotoracism ad.

I passed by him, too, clutching my copy
of Marx's *Capital*, with a divider between
pages that warned of a laborer's alienation.
A fevered World Cup in the theatre
of the unwanted.

II

The Video Assistant Referee was there, too.
And to witness the final acts of a dying match
is to unveil a fluttering of mirth in the heart,
palpitations that pound like the tiring legs of
a favored team in the ruins of a fading game.

As the ambience trembled with the wildness
of furious fans, the rumblings of dreamers
about to snatch a famous night at the Etihad,
a breathlessness descended elsewhere like a hush.

Nothing describes the cusp of a famous victory
like the eruption of emotions exploding on the faces
of underdogs in a frenzied search for a crowning
second in a field of dreams.

But a ball soon crossed a keeper's line, a goal
with the intricacies of a move that caught every
eye on after a pass of magic; a storm of silence
at stoppage time cast a spell on the stadium.

Atop a sound that whistled through the air
was the video assistant, a killjoy of sorts.

III

But he was not bothered, as he could not be,
his eyes emptied of the lights from the heaven
he helped to build.

Neither the victory goals nor the wages
of his toil could really be gained.

Passage of Time

Ever so often, time
glides in a sky full of stars,
a sky racing with drifting
clouds shaped like things
you once knew, things that
leave behind their fondest
shticks. You wonder
where your friends
have gone, where
yesterday's innocence
might yet be found,
or why tales
of sunshine become
long and weary nights
that haunt the rhythms
of life like a winter
without warmth.

You wonder why tiny
griefs become a flood,
why the clock ticks forever,
never looking back
to seize the wonders
that pass by, memories
of days you recall
with the resilience
of a watery eye.

You wonder what
twinkles from a loving
eye could have chased
you like a smitten lover
and ask: “where did
the years fly to?”

Just Struggle

What is familiar soon fades away—neither as
an untraveled path that peters out at night
when the sky kisses an eeriness from a distance
nor as a memory disappearing into a depth,
exploding into an afterlife of traumas,
but as a rebellion that purloins the sturdiest
desires, tethered to the brutal fictions
of perpetual becoming. Unarrived, and never
arriving, a deluge of hollows echoes through,
an obsidian nightmare on the protest ground
stands before the door of unfreedom. What
is familiar soon unravels into strangeness,
disappearing into a sail beyond the fetters
of terror, an unknown sea that terrifies not,
a place of refuge where dignity is Black power.

Beloved April

The trickles of spring rain
sometimes vex the winter-wearied,
but the sparkles of summer soon
come through the tree branches again,
bearing shining rays heralding hope
like the face of a suitor pining
for the magic of love requited.

And when summer's flowers linger
forever, unfurling in their softness,
with daises and asters blooming
in their graces, the leaves of Autumn
soon loom near, whispering the breeze
of melancholia, the unwanted goodbyes
that reunite us with the scarves
and toques of winter's warmth,
until a beloved April unwraps her leaves
in a fount that is not cruelty.

You lot have believed a lie. What
famous poet bespoke of rebirth as
a torture to the land when a month
returns the glow of nature, painting
the face of the earth with brushstrokes
and all that came before it?

The Taste of Tales

At night, my body dreams
of words, conjuring up stories

like the ghosts of memories
refusing to be forgotten.

The other day at Kreuzberg,
a döner kebab sent me

back to blissful edges of Lagos,
to the joys of party Jollof

and the tales we often tell of it
on the battlefields of Twitter feeds.

There is something about
the nighttime that flavors

the grammar of stories,
when dark skies and moonlit

fantasies are faithful witnesses
to the chronicles of taste.

At night, when the mind
awakens in a garden of words,

what feeds it cannot
be fathomed.

Ennui

Someone said we ought to call a thing
marred with ugliness by its proper name,
despair. But naming a thing, a heaviness
that floods your moments of joy does not
cancel it; for the emptiness lingers after
shallow dreams on the earth, as a mirage
in our hearts, appearing again as
the phantom of an uncertain reality;

another void, barren of the love
that once glistened like freshly fallen snow
on the sunny days we used to know;
sunny days—always beckoning—
and never leaving us unembraced.

The year we languished came upon
us as at other times before the plague;
it stole the colors from our canvas and
left us with a facade of smiling faces;
its ennui, the collective affect that eclipses
the light which was our path out of the void,
the crevices inside each of God's children.

Wraith Lord

Today the life you had
again recedes before us.
    Once more you had fled
    a face that walked into
    your house, a figure from
    the past you left long ago
    when the flood came
    like angry tides rushing
    men to their end.

"There's something about
him that puzzled us all," one of
your neighbors would later say of you,
wrestling with superstitions betraying
the logic of his cultured mind.

But you left so hurriedly
    that evening, a crab fleeing
    the ghosts of sea otters,
    vanished into the mystery that
    brought you at first into
    the circle of earthlings.

Now what remains is the myth
of your deeds, the apparitions
of the living we cannot embrace.

Wedding Cake

What becomes of a wedding cake
serving neither the pleasures of patrons
nor the appetites of merry crowds
that gather in reception halls with
geles and gaieties like a sky of colors?

That wedding cake is her own master,
the triple-layer of sweetness coated
in chocolate and cream, standing with
pride at the behest of her bride, hastening
to perfect the foreverness of friendship.
She surveys faces in sacred silence,
willing to give herself and melt
in the mouths of lovers and guests.

The cake, sacramental witness
to the mingling of vows from lips like
the collusion of rivers and fountains,
a record of hearts that finally shed
their frostiness, the outpour of unsayable
wishes by cynical gents, so too the long
stares of bridesmaids whispering
a jubilant envy in secret.

But that cake embraces her mission,
its dying moments, granting a couple
an entrance into life, a paradise they pray
not to be sundered. What becomes

of a wedding cake? Does she end up
on Instagram or pretend to behold
the madness of love floating
on the faces of two?

Truth

Winds of lies sometimes tear truth in halves:
reality disappearing like a puff of smoke
carried by the anger of gusts and raucous mobs.

What is left is a wake of what could have been
or what actually is, a simulacrum of the real.

> Like autumn trees in a garden without
> flowers, lacking leaves and fruits to boast,

until truth bursts back to us like a seed
erupting from a ground soaked in rainwater.

The reign of deceit may last a decade or more,
but the tongue of truth soon speaks,
taking back its velvet crown.

II

Willkommen

At the airport in Frankfurt, love won.
There you see a thing of beauty
in a rare place, a marvel to behold,
metaphors giggling and leaping like
the greetings of arrivals at airport gates,
when travelers are hailed by their folks at last.

Only the joys of kinship propel them;
soothing like a song that lulls to sleep
is the ebullience they exude after
an endless journey through the vastness
of a cerulean sky, through an expanse
of clouds and the monotony of cramped
legroom in economy class.

Home at last. Not geographies that gather
the mundane where tedium dreams of escape
from stories of everydayness, but the hearts
of lovers carrying flowers and kisses to the gates,
knowing the smiles and hugs that consign
them to a place.

Departures

There's no such thing as a temporary departure.
Every absence of the body plagues the places
left behind with longing, aches that escape as sighs.

And the muteness of empty spaces quakes with
the memories of times shared and gained, when
summer goes away, and yellow leaves begin to fall.

Yet, the hushed voices of a room merely echo
the prayers of lovers clinging to hardy roses
that dare seasons of exits and farewells.

Their ecstasies, once hushed by the silence
of departing feet, summon the promises we
made to remember each other when
togetherness is an elusive place to find.

Rites of Exit

By the door to the old Terminal
at MCI, they share spontaneous hugs
that linger on the faces of strangers
into an eternity of unwanted stares.
And tears, too. She knows he will come
back again when, he says, the flowers
are back in bloom, and kisses that warm
the lips return to grow a garden
in the heart again.

They cling to each other and
to the warmth of a dying moment,
each offering the other a chest
to melt into the gulf that threatens.

With eyes that glitter like sequins,
their goodbyes were said in silence,
the sunshine over them glinting
as tulips over the shadows that
fashioned their fears. She says
to him, "I miss you already," the tenor
of her voice, a whisper of love
in the ears of a passing audience.

A Parisian Journey

In Paris, you find a gentleman in a colored suit
that gleams with pride, his face staring into
the breasts of a flower seller on the Champs-Élysées.

The gait of his figure detains your eyes as you pass
him who doesn't see you or determines not to;
the flowers seduce his legs, calling away from
other passions, you think. Until he tumbles into
a pot—the begonias beside his choice belle dispersing
like elephant-eared leaves into a paradise of confusion.

There, the light passes through his dark sunglasses
into your sunken heart as you behold eyes that see not
and continue your lonesome journey through the city.

A Hand in Wiesbaden

The things we notice when strangeness calls
linger forever in the depths of the mind.

What the eyes behold when all is wired and
home is far endures beyond the doubts of now.

When Babel returns and threatens speech,
all that is left is a humanity that unites, yet veiled

to those who choose not to see others. Until
friends from a far country come along, placing

comfort upon our shoulders, a benign hand gesturing
to our weariness, "I, too, have trodden this path."

Heroes who wrestle us from the growing despair
that suffocates, who, going an extra mile, wait

like the Black woman at a Chicago station
until we have boarded the right train before

continuing on their own journey away from hell.
Heroes that speak an alien language but

carry the motley hands of a shared fragility.
The people we notice when strangeness calls

are those who plant love from a heart of kindness,
the ones who swear lifelong oaths to good deeds
and from a harvest of thorns seek the fallen seeds.

Amsterdam

At first, I didn't make much of Amsterdam,
my eyes set on the London sun,
that hoary crown of a faded empire.

Nothing stood out there I thought,
except ferries bidding tourists to ride
on ancient canals stretching into concentric
circles calling out to lovers.

Nothing stood out there I thought,
but the smile of a friend from Marrakesh
who enthused about tulips that bloom
in May and the museums housing the relics
of past and future desires.

The bicycles, too, little engines that will
a city to their power, entrancing the Dutch
whether in rain or shine, their riders caught
in a mad frenzy of haste.

The beauty of the place played forever
in my head yet I lacked words to describe it.
So too the sex museum by the central station.
I had walked past it wondering whether to go in
or walk away, a gentleman without his lady.

It seemed an easy decision for anyone
untethered to plans. Except that it wasn't.

A Train Conversation

There is something here to remember if, as a trained
eavesdropper without a room of your own, you are lured
to bend ears to the prattle of strangers on a speeding train.

Fellow guardians of wanderlust, their voices fill your coach
with a torrent of cascading words dripping with an echo you
love and despise at the same time, the whispers of ambivalence.

But a melancholia in their voices mingles with a sea of joy,
a gelatinous sadness masked by the glories of lores regaled.

Tales they tell in tongues untangle your own memories
of home and the many places you have lost and gained at once,
recollections of unread goodbye letters and unsmiling border
officers who collect your fingerprints without seeing you.

An Airbnb by East End

It is not every day we get the chance to know
ourselves and question what we know.

Like it happened on the road to Barking,
where fallen leaves, mushed together with rain,

adorned the path to my Airbnb room.
It was supposed to be a thing of beauty,

but a collage of decaying daisies
on dirty ground evoke stubborn memories.

As I judged the meanings of this faltering image,
I piled up the blame on the faces of bystanders,

each face that makes a home on my pathway,
not knowing their stories, the idioms of their struggles.

How quickly we forget the mutuality of our pains,
the ugliness that clings eternally to each of us who drinks

from the same slip-stream of warts and all.
Still, what startled the most was not my shallows

but the high-nosed verdict of a questioning voice:
whose heart is this that drains itself of wisdom?

Rain on a London Ride

Whether the souls on the District Line
tied themselves into nothingness,
I do not know; but of the daily rituals
of commuters in moments of enjambments
and stoppages, I see a thing: spaces where
words marry silences and the elements
outside, the unruliness of children
ecstatic in a playground muddle, sound
like the slipperiness of an impatient world.

Another glance: my eyes follow
the rhythms of eyes that fall into handhelds
as if to divine a path for the train through
the swirling of fingers; faces beholding
books that refuse to be read because
intruding pilgrims keep asking
what the next stop is.

Some of the eyes betray an indifference
so cold they arrest the stares of strangers
who look away to hide a voyeur's shyness.
Yet several more linger in the visions of other
passengers, pretending to look past the glass
window speeding past Putney Bridge.
An Afrobeat tune relieves my wandering
eyes; it sounds like Burna Boy, but I cannot

be too sure: the announcement of another
arriving station bellows from the speakers.

Ruffles and bodies collide in fleeting
moments of familiar tensions; they scamper
in and out of crowded coaches into the flooding
that awaits them. I make way for a black-eyed
girl; shoulders brush against each other;
the smell of her perfume wafts beside me
like the winds swelling the sail of a lurching vessel.

The wetness of a grey London sky
welcomes her as another warning to "mind
the gap between the train and the platform"
follows behind us. An umbrella goes
up as if beseeching ferocious petrichor
to steal through the open door.
A drop falls on my skin like raining acorns
in the Fall. I want to stay back to drink
my own reflection, but everyone keeps
exiting into a furious wetness, into
the aloneness of their journeys.

Cabin 6604

In Cabin 6604 on a train
clacking on a track to Montreal,
I am reading Fanon preach of violent
decolonization and enjoying
the mélange of city and country
that spreads out, farmhouses
and silos in the middle
of nowhere. With wintry winds
on its sail, the horse gallops,
charging along with a fury
that greets snow-painted fields
and frigid shrubs.

I overhear a trainee doctor
by my side tell a stranger
of the mother's dishes that
call her home to visit.
She struggles to contain
her Covid mask and the many
joys home may bring her way.

Something in her voice
reverberates like Moyo's
litanies, reaching from Lagos
as echoes of a mother
deprived of her son.
But when the driver
announces tickets

will be checked,
a side look tells
another tale:
the eternal
surveillance
of the Black man.

But even decolonial
fervor is sometimes
born of a gentleman's
agreement,
to Fanon's chagrin!

I want to write a poem
for this returning moment
and the angst of my immobility
in a moving railcar,
but a crew member
interrupts my thoughts
with a shout of her wares.
Her bazaar forbids
cash on the train,
only Visa cards
for those dreaming
of coffee and
something to bite.

As visions of stolen
lands speed into
memories of violence
in the face of another native,

capital, it was that had
the final laugh.
Or so it seemed.
Until my Uber driver,
freshly banned on Twitter,
arrived to chant
fuckeries to fascists!

A Jalamia in Berlin

In Berlin, you wake up to a sloppy
weather in the summer months,
the signs of a dawn that traps you
in a dither like a reluctant city
unable to decide if it wants
to rain or shine.

You know a city that delights
as it glides into a splash of sprawling
colors. Yet, its chaos pens haunting
memories threading the fabric
of its beauty from the dreams
of vanquished despots.

A beauty that composes
sonnets from the frenzy of unwanted
nostalgias, the manifestoes of former
hippies carrying strollers and backpacks
along walkways in gentrified Prenzlauer Berg.

What you remember most from
the heterotopias that swallow you
are the sights that take you home,
the döner kebabs that splash images
of Agege's bread and akara on your mind,
or the figure of the brother in a jellabiya
strolling by a corner around
a busy bahnhof.

He, too, transports you back to Lagos,
another city of dreams, where a lagoon
of laughter flows daily into rivulets
of uncertain pleasures.

III

Empty Streets

It's a Memorial Day weekend in Lawrence,
and I drive through empty streets—
Iowa deserted, stripped naked by the absence
of students gone home, like vagrant birds
filling the sky with whir and motion.
A few cars drive past. I wonder if I am
really driving or I am driven by a grief
unknown to the driver smiling at me
by a traffic light that halts the frenzy
of his Tesla.

Here I am, driven on an empty street,
thinking of Len, my teacher in Saskatoon
whose passing I just read about on Facebook.
As his voice gets wafted back from memories,
so do the goodbyes of a last email and the
deeds of a sage who lighted minds and
made them forgo a little learning for a harvest
of knowledge. And Jerry, a board member
at church who also left on Friday, a decade
short of a century. The feeble hands I shook
two Sundays ago, now cold and gone.

Here I am, driving on an empty street,
with a grief too distant to name, a grief that
eludes, not because I am neither kin to both
teacher and brother. Not because strangers
cannot feel pain when the colors of others

become dim and fall off like stars from
the heavens. Someday, every street will
become empty, and there will be none
to bear the burden of the grief that breaks
us all. For now, Memorial Day urges
a rememory of those who gave their lives
to free the sun to shine through the shadows
that remain with the rest of us. And it finds
me driving and being driven by the memories
of men who dwell in streets no longer empty.

Rebel Angels

Should we unfollow comrades who never
leave Twitter because they have left us?

A tweet waltzed upon my feeds last night,
one of the many jabs of a Montreal liberal.

Reposted by a guy mocking the victories
of #metoo from the glows of screens and hate.

"Let's stand up for justice," the tweet
screamed with a gracious fury that drained life

from the curated bravados of macho men
who grabbed the genitals of women and joked

about it in the locker rooms of fragile egos,
factories of farts and warts. But the owner

of that tweet isn't here anymore, nor are
the flames of the struggle they kept alive,

only memories of their wit and many clapback
and the profile picture of a woman reading Marx,

smiling like one in the company of rebel angels
contemplating the scenes of their former world.

Rumors of a Sloppy Kiss

I want to tell my daughter about the first girl
I kissed before I met her mother. Is she ready
for my tale? Will she hear words textured
by the voice of a repentant playboy or the nostalgias
of a man subdued by the passions of her mother?

As that girl and I poached a moment of innocence
neither of us truly knew, the look in her eyes
seemed to foretell a future that now demands
a confession for the thick fog of fear that threatened
the pleasures of youth.

But how do I tell my daughter that my first kiss
was a sea of sloppiness, a wetness for the shuddering
breath of two neophytes in a tango with naivety?

A Memorial Visit

That visit to the King Center was a trauma reopened,
the traumas of ancestors
whose dreams stubbornly flinch
from the past into the strictures that swallow us still.

What we witness in the sculptures
to memory does not unwind the past
nor repair the fractures in the *polis*.

Neither do the artifacts of remembering ever stay silent
though we trample upon them, as in those in Berlin,
or simply stand before them in a dark museum where
cameras are barred from clicking to the afterlives of terror.

What we witness in the sculptures to memory
is the spectacle of ancestors who broke leashes
that threatened their minds, elders still dreaming
of freedom as frozen eyes watching the breathless.

A memorial to the horror that stalks the present,
like zombies from the abyss of a violent history.

Remembering

Prague was the protagonist of it all.
The weight of memory laid siege
again to a wandering mind there,
an army enclosing the walls of an
ancient city. But that skirmish was
first in Bayreuth: in a Baroque Opera,
Margravial—awakened annually
by the sound of festival music
and the footfalls of tourists releasing
their camera shutters in pursuit of Bavaria,
its history. And Wagner's *Wahnfried*.
The marbles in those places brimmed
with earthy reds, the colors of opulence
dulled by the crumples of age; they called
out to you, asking of the monuments
you left at home: "What became of Benin
and Timbuktu and Zimbabwe, and
the pyramid of walls that unfolded
greatness?" I shrugged it aside, blaming
the brutalities of Empire, while scripting
indifference to truth. But their voices
never left me. What is it we lose
when we don't remember?
The same thing happened in Prague.
I was in Charles Square awaiting the magic
bells of the city's astronomical clock,
a Medieval fairytale that enchanted
the city of spires with magic and crowds.

In the cacophony of expectant faces looking
upwards to catch the spectacle of monks
and priests, in the brushing of strange bodies
flirting with time, the angel of history returned
to ask, “What is it we lose when
we don’t remember?” This time, the voices
stayed, a reminder of the elders at home
who labored to record their own days,
to ask what became of the chronicles
of their memories.

Tidal Waves

A tsunami of memories
    floods the heart every time our
    feet touch the shores
of other lands, a certain longing
for the places where we used to be,
    places that push us
to the eaves
    of new homes and discoveries,
to what we must now embrace
after a search of many skies,
the havens to which we aspire.

A tidal wave—
      a pendulum that
    swings our warring emotions
    back and forth
with whispers
    that echo new names.

Julie

. . . to whom I never said goodbye

Even now it hurts. To look back
hurts like being swallowed by the pain
in your eyes each time I walk away
from you. A spatulate tongue,
the panting sign of silent grief
chronicles the steps that veer off
without remorse.

You want to come with me,
but you must return home
to those with whom I share
your love, the cuddly pups that suck
at your breast and yelp at stray cats
from the neighbor's yard.

And with neither kennels nor sitters
nearby, only the dog butcher beckons,
returning a half-smoked cigarette
to smolder again between
lips stained with canine blood.

So, despite the sadness on your sail,
you hold your tail high in the air,
wagging stories of warmth like a flag
you wave to eternal friendship as you
return to the safety of lonesomeness.

Yet I must look away,
unable to hold back the tears
from a heart that wishes
you never leave.

A Dream of Rain

Last night I heard the sound of rain in my sleep.
The roofs in Lawrence welcomed a fury from above;
the wrath of it all flooded a wakeful mind with echoes
of Lagos, that city where petrichor heralds the end
of dryness as rain meeting the thirst of trees mixes
with the aromas of their leaves to spring into life
broken flowers marred by the touch of angry sunrays.

The rain in Lagos tricks the clouds; the rain in Lagos
drinks up the unruliness of grace, pouring without
libations to the ways of a maddening throng,
greeted by the wildness of children cupping their hands
to drink from the puddles mother forbade them to enter.

A monkey post soon seizes the gaze, a makeshift soccer
net receiving a rushing ball weighed down by a flow
that joins in a docile tributary to the street gutter.

On the Island, a Nollywood crew is rushing to save
a camera from a sudden surge. At Tejuosho, market women
defy the downpour, covering their wares like lovers
clinging to each other under fake rain in a movie scene.

But this shower touches the skin, a real stranger to the flea
market that abhors it; it visits again with patters vibrating
with the warmth of an anxious earth, as a tipsy rainbow
stretching its beauty into the chaos of a city's charm.
Last night a rain in Lagos dared to japa into my sleep.

IV

Undressing

A cluster of naked trees once stood
alone on a Christmas Eve. Along the frayed
edges of the pathway to a Rewe store
in Pankow, they stood dancing to the winds,
secluded from home. But it was a winter
without snow, when the park was barren,
the branches bare, and only
the chirping of festive birds filled the air.

As I walked past the trees, indifferent to
an undressing in front of some nude statues,
a dreamy couple leaning on each other's
breasts, a twig fell on my shoulder, a prompt
to the bareness of a being whose beauty is
fading but not faded.

Curiosity is a beautiful thing, I thought,
following the twig's descent into a dance
of dry leaves levitated by winds like
a dervish in mid-air.

In the Woods

Yesterday, as I labored up the hill
to Mount Oread, a squirrel seized
upon my amble in the woods,
scurrying around in weaves and leaps
like an athlete in a sprint for her last medal.

The quarrel rustled up by my weary
legs, and the frenzied gait of a scrunched
face soon became a truce, as each of us
went their own way, in search of
their vanities and nuts.

On Jayhawk Boulevard

As patches of green bloom again
on trees once unclothed on Jayhawk
Boulevard, a queen of the season
returns to unfurl her beauty into
them, serenading the eyes
in the annual parade of April's flowers,
serrated leaves, pointing skywards, sway
to the music that keeps the eye
on the flame of spring, a season that
softens frigid hearts, its soothing
like the calmness of rain.

I want to linger from my car and listen
to what the flowers whisper to the winds,
or what the Jayhawks dream about
in the hum of a Kansas Union overflowing
with the curse of busyness, but a loud honk
from the trucker behind interjects with a sound
from Hades. And I must abide the dictates of a busy
traffic that calls away from heaven's beauty.

Liquid Fires

The trees by my window shed their leaves again,
every fall a ballad for parting tales, every leaf
a message of seasons to come.

And here I stand, enthralled by a dance
of yellow dreams, between meadows of dryness
and the threat of wintry whispers, drinking
dregs from the sky's departing eye.

But the smell of rain soon comes,
the sudden scents of the earth after the weeks
of dryness. It mingles with warmth today, calling
forth a shower of memories that descends upon us
like a weatherman bearing tales from other worlds.

Rain, rain, come again. Never wait for some
other day. The land is drunk with burning fuels.

Old Wine

They say you might lose your
identity when your feet touch down
on a foreign land, but my father would
often bicker with that: "What we lose is not
just ourselves," he used to say to me.
Who you are may be sacred, for what can
redeem the immortal badges of the soul?
What we lose when we travel is the gift
of old friends, the wine that aged with us
when all was young and the petals of childhood
bade us smile. Neither Facebook chats
nor fresh leaves falling on the grounds of new
forests can atone for them. Yet the harvest
of innocence, the first fruits of our earliest
bonds, ever remains.

Seagulls

Because threnodies oft bring with them
a presence you don't want to feel or feed,
we miss the season of the shorelines:
salt water, crashing waves, and cawing
seagulls that steal a sandwich by the waters.
Those who ponder not the beauty of the coastlines
miss the rhythms that silence many storms.

Yet the seagulls never tire of their swooping,
a band that glides a flash of freedom
into daydreams, with sparkles that ripple across
grey skies. To swim in these waters is to bear
a majesty that puzzles.

Loving a Feeling

Maybe she will crawl underneath the moon again
when we all love her whom everybody hates to love—

the house cat that purrs endlessly as one
both yearning for our touch and in deep contemplations
of our scorn; with eyes that glow in the engulfing night,
pouncing forever upon our angst, banished indoors.

Her only wish is to snuggle in our warmth,
to hold us in the spell of her affections
and mumble meows that pine to catch birds and mice.
But our fear of the unknown constrains her graces.

Butterflies

A flowing river flutters
before us like a butterfly
leaping in the winds for the sweetness
that awaits it;

the skies we share unfold a triumph
of nectars; they mirror waters
bidding us to where we hear
what the rivulets have to say.

Will their words stay between us
or will they stray on the back
of a whirlwind slapping a prayer
of innocence on the face of nature?

The other day I sought silence in the wild
and heard the earth rain down stories
on those whose ears go up, where
the butterfly returns to find her pollen
again and us in each other's arms.

A Fall to Desire

Fall in Lawrence is a spectacle
that sheds its greenness
into a carpet of falling leaves
bearing glints of red in the sun,
a scattering that dances
to the winds, smelling like
pumpkin pie from
the Walmart at 6th.

The colors adorn the streets
like curls of crimson dancing
in the breeze, seedless
maples telling tales
of nature's beauties.

Yet, the sun over Oread
lingers and pipes a song
for a flâneur's feet as he hastens
towards Thanksgiving to harvest
the laughter of friends.

You can tell what the season
blooms by the delights
of its brushstrokes on the faces
of the city's hills.

V

The Heart Is Where Home Is

"Bàbá, am I Nigerian?" asked she
that came the day a November snowstorm
engulfed Saskatoon, blanketing the prairies
with fury, a familiar avalanche that climaxed
into the cries of birth pangs.

"Yes, but you are also from Abeòkúta,"
Bàbá's voice rattles like the unsureness
that follows a migrant around when
home is the past a father loses to gain
himself, the future of childhood daydreams.

"Maybe we'll return to Nigeria someday?"
Bàbá wanted her to ask. Ọlọgbon ọmọ
ní ḿmú inú-u bàbá e dùn. "Yes, maybe,"
a readied answer for a child that gladdens
the heart through an unrolling of yesteryears.

But she walked away, returning to
the waffles on the table, and the burden
of a silence as inscrutable as the lines
of a difficult poem from a distant country.

The Tenderness of Friends

Nobody knows tenderness
like a man to whom it is a stranger.
He knows what he has never felt,
a feeling that eludes him like the words
that unbutton his silence, the struggle
to shed his mind in front of those
who misunderstand him from a far city
founded by the sages of indifference.

The tendrils of his anguish, strung
by a refusal to play the gallery's tunes,
bear sweetened fruits on a soil turned
to the blues of animus, a fierceness that
roars, a mystery that spirals from friends
who bleed both reds and roses like
a dehiscent wound on a sturdy leg.

Plinths of an agony for him who
knows tenderness like the back of some
roughened palms, for him misbegotten
by the affections of friendly fires.

Register Here, the Zoom Days

A requiem for the days spent on Zoom,
when each webinar was a world of tales,
a Webex of lies for the community online.
For the dreariness that swathed fatigued faces
In front of computer screens, and the colors
of a promise that dies in infancy, a refrain more
frequent than the bomber's fear. As you sing
threnodies in virtual lifeworlds boasting a sea
of knowledge, your mind yields to the otherworldly
power, clicks that rue the artificiality of
communions without mourning. And when
with awkward silence others welcome you,
or the more eerie goodbye after every last
word has been spoken, you pine for
the reel world of the thumb.

Desiring Dews

A warm stream rolls forever from their dimples,
summonsed by the kindest fires flowing through.
As Epicurean brooks gush into unruly bodies,
a ripple of new moons surges from blended lips—

neither the lurches of a hollow heart nor the swaying
of a beloved in empty winds but as a radiance cutting
across troubled waters like love that glides past foibles
into excesses, into foibles as a dance in a rain of desires.

To wash in it and yet wish for it, the eternal yearning
of the soul for its own honeycomb. Sometimes adrift
in an ocean of vain desires, yet caressing the wetness
that melts into memories.

The Second Commandment

I search for answers in the footage
of a parent screaming to the void
after learning their fifth grader was no more;
I search in the tears of teens carrying scars
from an earlier shooting in Florida,
the world crashing in on them,
as memories of an AR-15 orgy gather,
clouds in a night storm.

Another image comes on the screen:
the steps of tiny feet summoned
by fear into a fuzzy line like stars
that refuse to align, led in morbid silence
away from the scene of familiar crossfires,
the slaughterhouse of dreams a freedom
fighter must now defend with empty
thoughts and empty prayers on Twitter,
that vacuous agora of vain aversions.

Soon the scales cascade off the eyes:
To be free in America is to be fettered
to our guns; the second commandment—
an illusion of grandeur, the first, an annual
offering of blood to lobbyists in Washington.
Not even the pallbearer can abide the death
of common sense. How does a child die
on the altar of politics?

Immigrant Blues

I

To be an immigrant is to be a human
walking again in the footpaths of those
who trod the earth that was kin, to tread
the path of ancestors you do not know,
their dreams, their desires. And to run
with the winds that carried them
to the flames of other suns when
home became a cantonment
discharging old grenades that pursued
your neighbors into a lagoon brimming
with murderous water hyacinths.

To be an immigrant is to bask
in the tireless afterglows of people
passing by and leaving questions behind,
to harvest meanings from the signs of tireless
stares saying volumes of unsayable things.

To endure journeys that never end,
the constant dreams of succor elsewhere.

II

I saw the other side of love
One morning a plain-clothed
officer knocked on my door.
He bellowed for my green card,
the foreigner's claim to a slice

of a dream that loiters as nightmare,
desired, the apparitions of those
for whom home forever recedes
after crossing many rivers.

With a baldness surrounded
by scanty hair greyed by apathy
and a smiling face to guide his questions,
"Please show me your card, ma'am,"
he squealed to a bewildered mind,
the daughter of the harangued in the golden
city of freedom's empire.

Unfazed by a tongue-tied stillness
that heralds my pleas and stuttering lips,
he summoned his clubbers, and a series
of "open up" filled the air like
caterwauls of "America first" in a MAGA
rally on Fox News.

When my words finally forced their way,
it wasn't the ghosts of ICE that startled
the most. Nor the promises of cages
along the border or the barks of angry
dogs sniffing the bodies of children.

But the face of Emeka—whose legs
gathered a storm as he flew the house
the other night: did he mention my name
in the dark clouds that followed him?

A Valentine Poem

That story about wayward canticles
from love books came from a tongue dripping
honey and tales of exits. A day you are not here
is a shameless moment of longing. You ask
why the heart still pines for the muse it daily
seeks like a bee her honeycombs. You wonder
why absence repels like an unwanted friend
visiting in the heat of an ungodly hour, a moment
that dithers and forbids unravelling its next
passages. You wonder. So when I said,
"To love you is to bear you in my breast
even when you are not here," a feeling growls
inside of me and stretches into a sky where,
not holding you, I'm stuck to smiles shared
a flurry of seconds ago, memories crafted
by affections into a bouquet freshly plucked
from gardens that elicit longings, the magnolias
of passions. To be away from you is to become
a dry fountain. A day lingers into eternity
when you are not here.

Home Whispers Your Name

What binds the heart to places
are not the accoutrements
collected to make journeys
a deluge of happiness streaming
with endless chuckles.

What binds us to the spaces
we once cherished are the faces
that glitter as iridescence,
warming the soul, whose memories
transport us back as brushstrokes
splashing colors to other planets.

For what we truly lose when
we turn our back on home
is community, the people
that make the far country
a mirror to a dance of desires
on the dappled skies of lands
trimmed and tackled yet left behind;

a community forever fractured
but gained in the passing smiles
of strangers who dare to see
us from the majestic pinnacles
of their blindfolded visions.

What binds the hearts to places
are the mortals who become sullen
with a fleetingness of beauty and warts
reminding us of our own faces.

The Stars over Lagos

The stars over Lagos say cryptic things
at night. They beam their smiles over those
who meditate upon the face of the universe, like
children under the spell of a stubborn moonbeam.

They say the city does not write about running
brooks nor script coital lullabies for creaking beds
sung as a refrain to roses dreaming of fire
in a garden of two. They say the city does not sing
seaside laughter nor the pleasures of jollof beef
melting in the mouth as buttered rice in a plate.

Only the sound of dirges ricocheting off the darker
evenings of endless grief. Only the gongs of gulags,
the sound of chains to hands with hope in their heart.

But not so tonight, for the eyes ascend like falconers
soaring to the summit that foretells the glides of
a different muse. Not so this night of crimson stars
bestriding the skies like the Colossus of Lagos.
Not so tonight when the stars over us whisper
their names to the heads raised to the light above.

8th Season of Forever . . .

The sun shines from her face, not like
timid graces that tremble in the eye,
but as bright blushing from Venus
and shy rays that glow as the lights
of a starry night.
A lover festoons
her neck with desires, fiery yet soothing,
                    and a heart palpitates, waves in an ocean
                    of emotions; their lips touch like the beaks
                    of two swans facing each other in the heart
                    of a chill sea after a storm. Nothing there
is without the fury of love. Nothing dares
to tame a growing intensity save the bliss
of everyday monotonies threatening to call
away from the splendor being shared.

The Elysian Graces

of a pose compare to a geranium's bloom;
the gems to pluck off her cheeks sparkle
as sequins, stars from a sky of marbles.
So we melt into each other, whispering
tales that linger into an eternity of rainbows.

A tapestry of the imperfect, perfected
in the drapes of God, as heartbeats become
a communion of laughter. Every bone, a prayer

for brighter blooms. This serenade will be sung
evermore, to satiate a paradise of thirsts and
the colliding of bodies at night.

These lines are for Shade, the best of belles
in Ebenezer Obey's lyrics, and to whom
I said "I do" many seasons ago. And still do.

I Know Why Flames Have No Shadows

The sparks we left behind bear the flames
that keep the gods alive, like an ambrosia
of passions that linger forever atop lighted
candles on the table of forgotten desires.

They flicker as starlites, burning like
the softness. of a night smile after the storm
beneath the sheets. Our flames left no shadows
as they receded, the tide of a sea merging into
a coitus with their own fire.

JAMES YÉKÚ is a Nigerian-Canadian writer who lived in Saskatoon for six years before moving to Lawrence, Kansas, where he is an Assistant Professor of African Digital Humanities at the University of Kansas. He teaches introductory courses in African studies, Black masculinities, and digital literary studies. Yeku's poetry and fiction have been recognized with awards and nominations, including the University of Ibadan Okigbo Poetry Prize in 2008 (First runner-up).

"Although the politics of my Nigerian homeland animate several of the poems, their most abiding rumination is on the poetic space in which I have attempted to enunciate the constancy of change and the disruption of fixities. The intersections of the human experiences become evident in poems that make legible how enduring the harsh realities of winter storms and frost bites remind me of the adversities of home that so traumatize you that you feel the best gestures of love must be from afar."